Sometimes I Get So Angry!

ANGER MANAGEMENT FOR EVERYONE

Written by
David A. Anderson, Ph.D.

Illustrated by
Paul Sirimongkhon

PENSIVE
PRESS

Published by Pensive Press, LLC
www.PensivePress.com
Danville, Kentucky

ISBN 10: 0-9709057-1-8
ISBN 13: 978-0-9709057-1-0

Library of Congress
Control Number: 2006928175

For permission to use material from this
book, please contact the author at
Centre College
600 W. Walnut Street
Danville, KY 40422
Tel (859) 238-5282

For information on the art of
Paul Sirimongkhon, visit
http://web.centre.edu/phnom/ps.art/

Printed in the United States of America
by RJ Communications, LLC

To those who have suffered as a result of damaging emotions,
and to those with the willpower to overcome them

Forward

Unfortunate responses to negative emotions too often include violence and depression. In 2005, Americans experienced over 9,000 hate crimes, 16,000 murders, 30,000 suicides, and 5.2 million crimes of violence. Many more acts of uncontrolled anger, including domestic abuse, road rage, and workplace violence, go unreported each year. The purpose of this book is to present ten simple-but-effective alternative responses to negative emotions in a memorable way. It is our hope that these types of approaches will become better known and more frequently adopted.

Although it is normal to experience feelings of anger, it is worthwhile for everyone to explore ways to work through anger and other difficult emotions before they become explosive. The methods suggested in this book are just the tip of the iceberg. Some people benefit from writing down their thoughts or repeating expressions such as "it's alright" or "take it easy." Some people are calmed by music. Meditation, yoga, humor, hobbies, and sports can all be effective ways to blow off steam. Sometimes it is appropriate to seek professional counseling. The important thing is for each individual to find his or her own healthy way of dealing with anger and practice it diligently.

Note: Contrary to conventional wisdom, studies have shown that punching pillows, yelling, and similar forms of venting can stir up emotions rather than calming them.

More information on anger management is available online at www.apa.org/topics/controlanger.html, www.angriesout.com, and www.safeyouth.org/scripts/teens/anger.asp.

SOMETIMES I GET SO ANGRY
I COULD SCREAM!

BUT INSTEAD
I DRAW PICTURES OF
BETTER DAYS AHEAD
AND I FEEL
MUCH BETTER.

SOMETIMES I GET SO FURIOUS
I TURN RED!

BUT THEN I THINK ABOUT
A PLACE WHERE I
ALWAYS FEEL HAPPY
AND I FEEL
MUCH BETTER.

SOMETIMES I GET
SO FRUSTRATED BY A PROBLEM
I COULD BREAK SOMETHING!

BUT INSTEAD
I CONSIDER WHETHER
THE PROBLEM WILL
MATTER IN A YEAR.
IT USUALLY WON'T,
AND I FEEL
MUCH BETTER.

SOMETIMES I GET SO EMBARRASSED I COULD FEEL BLUE ALL DAY!

BUT THEN I REMEMBER
THAT EVERYONE MAKES
MANY, MANY MISTAKES,
AND THAT WE LEARN
FROM THESE MISTAKES,
AND I FEEL MUCH BETTER.

SOMETIMES I GET SO JEALOUS OF
WHAT SOMEONE ELSE HAS
I COULD RUIN A FRIENDSHIP!

BUT THEN I MAKE A LIST OF ALL THE THINGS I'M LUCKY TO HAVE AND I FEEL MUCH BETTER.

SOMETIMES I GET
SO IRRITATED
I COULD LOSE MY COOL!

BUT THEN
I STOP
MYSELF
AND
COUNT
TO TEN

AND I
FEEL
MUCH
BETTER.

SOMETIMES I FEEL SO UPSET
I COULD HAVE A TEMPER TANTRUM!

BUT THEN
I TAKE
SEVERAL
SLOW, DEEP
BREATHS

AND
I FEEL
MUCH
BETTER.

SOMETIMES I GET SO AGITATED
I COULD SAY THE WRONG THING!

BUT THEN I WALK AWAY
AND SING MY
FAVORITE SONG
AND I FEEL
MUCH BETTER.

SOMETIMES I GET SO MAD
I COULD HURT SOMEONE!

BUT THEN I TAKE MY
THOUGHTS OUTSIDE
AND GET SOME
EXERCISE AND
FRESH AIR AND
I FEEL MUCH BETTER.

SOMETIMES I GET SO BOTHERED I COULD HATE A GROUP OF PEOPLE!

BUT THEN I IMAGINE MYSELF AS A MEMBER OF THAT GROUP, AND I BEGIN TO UNDERSTAND THEIR BEHAVIOR, AND I SEE THAT MY ENEMIES COULD BE MY FRIENDS.

WHEN I DEAL
WITH MY FEELINGS
IN THESE WAYS,
I FIND THAT MY FAMILY
AND MY FRIENDS
AND MY LIFE
ARE MUCH HAPPIER!

Exercises

1. Shout "You didn't pick up your clothes!" Now whisper "You didn't pick up your clothes." Now shout and then whisper another expression that you might find yourself shouting often. If whispering helps you calm your emotions, consider whispering to express yourself when you're angry. You might also find that whispering is less likely to set other people off.

2. Write down three sources of anger in your life.
   a. Think about the first source and then take a brief walk outside.
   b. Think about the second source and then take a few deep breaths.
   c. Think about the third source and then hum your favorite song.
   Indicate which of these three approaches felt the best to you.

3. Write down an inappropriate way in which you have responded to anger in the past. Think about how you felt at the moment when you responded in that way, and describe an alternative, healthy approach that you could have adopted instead.

4. Try drawing a picture of a place that makes you happy. Visit this place often, whether in reality or in your thoughts.

5. It is important not to simply dismiss negative emotions. Write a few sentences about healthy ways to approach, not suppress, strong negative emotions including frustration, embarrassment, and hatred.

6. Make a happy expression with your face. Make an angry face. Can you feel the emotions your face is expressing? Consider how you can use your face and other body language to help yourself and other people feel more comfortable. Make a happy face again. Hold it. Hold it ...

Discussion Questions

1. What situations from your own life did the book remind you of?

2. Which of the ideas for how to handle negative emotions did you like the most?

3. Which of the emotions mentioned in this book do you feel the most often?

4. Can you tell when you're about to lose control of your emotions? What are the warning signs?

5. How do you usually deal with anger? Have you dealt with anger in ways that you regret?

6. What do you do when you're feeling embarrassed?

7. What calms you when you're feeling upset?

8. In what ways have others hurt you in their expressions of anger?

9. Do your parents or other role models have ways of handling anger that you admire?

10. Where is your "happy place"--a place where you usually feel happy?
    Do you keep that place in your thoughts when you are feeling unhappy?

Phnomphone (Paul) Sirimongkhon, a native of Vientiane, Laos, fled the communist regime with his family in 1975. He lived in Australia, Thailand, and France before arriving in the United States in 1979 to attend Berea College. He is now settled in Danville, Kentucky with his college sweetheart and their two boys. He is an abstract artist and has held numerous solo art exhibits. Aside from commissioned work, his recent projects include the artwork for the 2004 Kentucky Derby magazine cover, the 2006 Great American Brass Band Festival poster, and the cover art for another of Dr. Anderson's books. He also owns a skateboard shop and works full time as a graphic designer for Centre College.

David A. Anderson is the Paul G. Blazer Associate Professor of Economics at Centre College. He received his B.A. at the University of Michigan and his M.A. and Ph.D. at Duke University. His research on crime suggests that harsher punishments are unlikely to be effective deterrents to existing violence.[1] His conclusion, that the best way to address destructive emotions may be to promote greater awareness of anger management techniques, was the impetus for this book. He lives in Danville, Kentucky with his wife, son, and daughter. He and his family enjoy long-distance running as their favorite remedy for anger and stress.

---

1 See "The Deterrence Hypothesis and Picking Pockets at the Pickpocket's Hanging," 4:2 *American Law and Economics Review* (Fall, 2002) 295-313.